Break the Cycle:

A Practical Guide to Healing Generational Trauma, Crafting Your Parenting Legacy, Ending Reactive Parenting and Raising Confident, Emotionally Secure Kids

The Hidden Marketers of Childhood

Published by: Monique corker

Copyright © 2025 All rights reserved

No part of this publication may be copied, reproduced in any format, by any means, electronic or otherwise, without prior consent from the copyright owner and publisher of this book.

Dedication

To my beloved grandmother, Carrie B. Lovette, affectionately known as Baby who I will always love for her showing me unconditional love; my mother, Michelle Fort who I admire and love for her strength; my father, Guerian Fort who stepped up to the plate to show me fatherly love; my sister and brother who have been there with me through thick and thin; and most importantly, my loving husband, Derrick Corker, and my two children who are my heartbeats and who inspired me to write this book. You have witnessed the realities I share here, and I hope this work helps others break generational cycles and dispel the myth of forgetting.

Acknowledgments

Writing this book has been one of the most transformative journeys of my life. Every word comes from a place of deep reflection, personal growth, and an unwavering desire to make a difference. While I wrote this book in its entirety, I used AI as a resource to assist in generating ideas, references, and supporting content, which I then curated, edited, and developed to align with my vision and voice.

To my family, friends, and all those who inspired me along the way—thank you for your encouragement, honesty, and love. This book is a testament to the lessons we learn from life, the resilience we find within ourselves, and the legacy we create for our children.

Table of Contents

Introduction: The Hidden Marketers of Childhood

CHAPTER 1: The Myth of Forgetting

CHAPTER 2: "I Turned Out Fine" – Authority Bias in Parenting

CHAPTER 3: The Power of the First Five Years

CHAPTER 4: Yelling, Arguing, and Emotional Regulation

CHAPTER 5: My Achilles Heel: Money, Spending, and the Mask of Insecurity

CHAPTER 6: The Role of Grandparents and Extended Family

CHAPTER 7: Single Parenting – Building Bridges, Not Walls

CHAPTER 8: Projections and the Weight of the Past

CHAPTER 9: The Intersection of Religion, Values, and Parenting

CHAPTER 10: The Parent Relaunch – Designing Your Positive Parenting Campaign

Bonus Chapter: The Unseen Curriculum – Modeling Life Beyond Parenting

Bonus Section: The Parenting Toolbox – Resources for Success

BREAK THE CYCLE

Your Family's Name

Introduction: The Hidden Marketers of Childhood

I remember saying as a child, "I will not grow up and be like my mom." What I knew back then was simple: I didn't want to yell at my kids when I became a parent. My mom was a great provider and a woman I admired deeply. But at times, it felt like another person would take over—almost like an alien figure had invaded her body, transforming her into someone so mean and unrecognizable. Those moments left me questioning how the same woman who could provide so much love and stability could also create such fear and confusion.

The yelling never truly allowed me to grasp the overall message. In my mom's eyes, it probably got my attention, but I often wonder if she ever paused to think, "Am I teaching, or am I simply forcing a behavior?" Now, as an adult, I've come to firmly believe that teaching a behavior is far more effective than forcing one. The latter doesn't just create resistance; it fosters resentment and triggers the fight-or-flight response, leaving lasting emotional imprints.

How often do we as adults say, "The message was lost in the delivery"? For me, that statement became painfully clear as I navigated my own journey as a parent. Despite my childhood vow, I found myself falling into the same patterns—because yelling was all I knew, and it came naturally. I also forced myself to believe it was better than traditional spanking or punishment by taking away things or isolation.

As parents, we are the architects of our children's environment—shaping both their internal world, like their sense of self, and their external behavior, how they interact with others. In the beginning, we hold so much control over how they perceive themselves and the world around them. For example, when I was a child, I was placed in a constant state of fear when we went out in public. I knew I shouldn't speak unless spoken to, shouldn't ask for anything, and certainly shouldn't act out. At home, I was often reminded to "stay in a child's place." These conflicting expectations left a gap in my ability to process how I was supposed to act or interact as I grew older.

This dynamic isn't just about what we say to our kids—it's about what they observe. When children see adults yelling at each other or arguing over something trivial, like a parking space, it sets an unconscious tone. They start to think, "Oh, this is how I should handle frustration." Even witnessing an adult snap at a cashier or lose their temper in a moment of stress becomes a silent lesson in how to respond to challenges.

And yes, I know not everyone will agree with me on this, and that's okay. I'm not trying to speak to everyone. I'm speaking to the ones who are ready to peel back the layers of their parenting, no matter how much hurt or discomfort it might reveal. This isn't about assigning blame or dwelling on past mistakes—it's about understanding the unintentional patterns we've inherited and passed down.

If we're willing to take an honest look, we might realize that some of the communication struggles our kids face—hesitating to speak up, struggling to express themselves, or reacting with anger—can be traced back to the environment we created, often unintentionally. The truth is, we can't force a child to close their mouth when it's convenient for us and then hope they'll magically learn how to hold thoughtful, confident conversations later in life. Children need consistency, safe spaces, and opportunities to practice communication if we want them to excel in it. It begins with us modeling the very behaviors we want our children to carry forward, dismantling the outdated mantra of "Do as I say, not as I do."

Every word we say, every action we take, and every habit we model creates a blueprint for how they will interact with the world. If that environment is filled with arguing, yelling, or negativity, our children are likely to replicate those behaviors, believing they are the norm. Even more, children begin to forecast what they don't like about us as parents, using those reflections to vow they won't become like us.

Sound familiar? Many of us have said the same thing, only to later realize we inherited—and passed on—patterns we thought we'd left behind.

Think About This:

Reflect on a moment when you noticed your child imitating you—a phrase they picked up, a habit they mirrored, or even the way they responded to frustration. Children are like sponges, soaking up not just what we intentionally teach them but everything we model through our behavior. It's easy for us as parents to use our authority to force children not to mimic us but the truth is they are simply mini reflections of what we have shown them. No one likes to see the uglier side of themselves, but our kids are usually the first to show us who we really are.

I'll never forget an elementary teacher once telling me, "I can learn so much about a household just by watching the children." She explained how kids mimic arguing, yelling, or sometimes joyous moments without embarrassment. To them, it's normal behavior—a reflection of the world they know. In their innocence, they almost wear these behaviors like a badge of honor, a rite of passage shaped by their home environment.

Here's the Marketing Touch

It wasn't until I began reflecting on my own habits—and drawing from my background in marketing—that I realized the striking similarities between parenting and marketing. I'm embarrassed to admit that this reflection was prompted in part by some brutally honest feedback from my own kids as they reached 18 and beyond. They shared the conversation no parent wants to hear: "You were an amazing mom, but you also traumatized me." That moment was a wake-up call, reminding me of the importance of paying attention to feedback—whether it's verbal or the subtle, nonverbal clues our children give us every day.

With a master's in marketing, I've studied how repetition and consistent messaging create brand loyalty. I've also learned the importance of understanding my audience, knowing what I want them to experience, and crafting that experience from a place of genuine connection—not through the equivalent of a forced sale that only happens when something is discounted. Repeated exposure to a product or behavior builds familiarity, and familiarity fosters adoption.

The same principle applies to parenting. Children internalize the behaviors they repeatedly observe—whether healthy or toxic—and these behaviors become the foundation for what they perceive as "normal."

Your Journey Ahead

As you read this book, you'll notice recurring marketing principles like repetition, authority, and emotional connection woven into the parenting journey. These parallels are not just theoretical—they're actionable. This is not a book about perfection; it's about awareness. It's about breaking free from the marketing-like campaigns we run unintentionally—campaigns filled with yelling, negativity, or neglect—and instead creating intentional, nurturing messages for our children to internalize brand inheritance of intentions.

A Series for Change

This book is just the beginning. Break the Cycle as it lays the foundation by exploring the impact of repeated patterns in parenting. But the journey doesn't stop here.
In the next book, **Break the Cycle-What They See Is Who They'll Be**, will go deeper into how our actions influence their friendships, authority, and habits.
Then, in **Break the Cycle-The Hidden Curriculum of Parenting**, we'll uncover the unspoken lessons shaping their identities and values.
Together, this series will guide you towards a more intentional approach to parenting—one step at a time.

Becoming the Marketer of Your Legacy

Parenting isn't about being perfect; it's about progress. So, let's start here—by becoming the marketers of the kind of legacy we want to leave for our children.

CHAPTER 1: The Myth of Forgetting

As parents, we sometimes cling to the hope that children are too young to remember our mistakes. It's comforting to believe that the yelling, the tension, or the hurried "not now" moments won't stick with them. But the truth? They always do. I have heard countless people including celebrities or influencers who speak on the past trauma from how they were raised. I'm not trying to paint a picture that everyone who deals with these things as kids will have issues because there are some people who are able to fully function with no strings attached from their past. I just wasn't that lucky and there are a lot of other unlucky adults with inner kid trauma out there to.

I learned this lesson the hard way—not just from my own experiences as a parent but from listening to young people recount the emotional scars they carry from their childhoods. Middle, High and even college kids have shared how the comments they overheard during a heated argument caused them anxiety, or the times they felt overlooked because everyone was rushing due to poor planning, or the moments when they sensed the stress their parents thought they were hiding. These memories stick either buried or at the surface but in some form or fashion will eventually reveal themselves to the world when we least expect it.

This book is about breaking free from those harmful patterns and finally giving ourselves a hard look in the mirror but with grace and mercy. It's about becoming aware of the messages we send our kids through our words, actions, and unspoken energy. It's not about being a perfect parent—it's about being intentional, mindful, and willing to grow.

Parenting in Action:

Think about a child who witnesses constant arguing at home. Over time, this becomes their "normal." As adults, they may struggle with conflict resolution, mirroring the behaviors they grew up with because it's all they know.

The Parenting Parallel:

Repetition in marketing builds familiarity and loyalty. Children, too, absorb repeated behaviors and internalize them as truths. Just as a repeated ad slogan sticks in our heads, repeated behaviors form the foundation of a child's understanding of the world.

Similarly, repeated parental behaviors become ingrained in a child's emotional framework, shaping their sense of self-worth and security or also propelling the I won't be like this comment when I grow up.

Your Next Step:

Choose one positive habit to repeat daily with your child, such as saying "I love you" before bed or asking about their day. It seems simple to you, but it's not only building consistency it is fostering a safe space and a different way of showing your love and affection.

Reflect on This:

Think back to your own childhood. What small moments stand out to you, for better or worse? How did they shape who you are today?

Reflect on a repetitive behavior you display—what message does it send? What feedback have you received from friends, coworkers, or bosses that, if you're truly honest with yourself, are rooted in how you were raised? It's comforting to believe that children are too young to remember the mistakes we make as parents. But the truth is, they do remember—not in exact words or events, but in the emotions and patterns we instill through repetition. These patterns become their blueprint, their emotional DNA.

Now, imagine a beautiful home constructed with unstable materials. No matter how often you reassure it or yelled at it, "You can withstand any storm," eventually, it will crumble under bad weather. The only option left is to rebuild—often from the ground up. Ironically, the same is true for humans. When we are built with emotional "materials" that lack stability, we're expected to grow into strong, resilient adults, surpassing the generation before us. This expectation is deeply ingrained in parenting—almost as if it's the foundation of our message to our children: "You have to be better than me."

While well-intentioned, this mindset often places an immense burden on children to outshine their parents' struggles without equipping them with the tools or stability to do so. It's a powerful yet paradoxical narrative—one that acknowledges our imperfections while demanding that our children rise above them. The question becomes: are we truly preparing them for that ascent, or are we merely projecting our unfulfilled aspirations onto their journey?

Our unintentional projected flaws cause years of future damage, and the process of correcting foundational flaws is costly, time-consuming, and often feels overwhelming or even impossible. This is why preventive parenting—laying strong emotional foundations from the start—is so much more effective than reactive parenting, which attempts to repair the damage later or leaves it up to hope that there is nothing to repair at all.

Unfortunately, our world seems subconsciously programmed to prioritize reaction over prevention. We wait for the cracks to appear before addressing the root cause, whether in our personal lives, families, or even larger societal systems. But the truth is, by investing in intentional, proactive parenting, we can avoid many of these cracks altogether. We can create a legacy of resilience, emotional health, and self-awareness that doesn't require costly repairs.

A parent once shared with me that her child consistently avoided bedtime stories. It wasn't until they worked on their nightly routine that the child admitted, "You're always rushing. I thought you didn't want to read with me."

Emotional Intelligence (EI) Insight: Navigating Repetition in Parenting

Repetition in parenting isn't just about actions—it's about the emotional tone and patterns we establish. With Emotional Intelligence (EI), parents can become more aware of the unintentional cycles they reinforce and work to replace them with nurturing habits. These shifts create an emotional environment where children feel secure, valued, and confident. Almost the same things we as adults EXPECT from everyone including our partners, our jobs, our friends etc.

Common Repeated Messages and Their Emotional Impact: Ignoring Emotional Needs:

Skipping small moments of connection, like failing to acknowledge a child's enthusiasm for their drawings, sends an unintended message: "Your feelings don't matter." Over time, this erodes trust and creates emotional distance.

EI Application:
Pause and fully engage in small moments, even if brief. A simple, "Wow, tell me more about this," can affirm your child's worth.

Dismissing Feelings:
Consistently saying, "You're fine" or "Stop crying" when a child is upset can teach them to suppress emotions rather than process them.

EI Application:
Use empathy to validate your child's feelings: "I see you're upset. Let's talk about what's bothering you."

Overpraising or Criticizing:
Excessive praise like, "You're the best at everything!" or harsh criticism like, "Why can't you get this right?" creates an unbalanced sense of self-worth.

EI Application:
Focus on effort and growth. Instead of general praise or criticism, try: "I noticed how much effort you put into this—it's impressive."

Why EI Matters in Repetition:
Repeated interactions, whether intentional or not, become the foundation of a child's emotional framework. Emotional Intelligence allows parents to pause, reflect, and adjust these patterns to foster healthier connections. By practicing empathy, self-awareness, and intentional communication, parents can

ensure their repeated actions nurture resilience and self-esteem helping to fuel their kids for a better adulthood.

Research from the Center on the Developing Child at Harvard University reveals that repetition during early childhood plays a crucial role in strengthening neural pathways. These consistent, positive interactions create a foundation for healthy emotional and cognitive development, shaping how children grow and thrive (Center on the Developing Child, n.d.)

Chapter 2: "I Turned Out Fine" – Authority Bias in Parenting

Many parents justify their choices with the phrase, "Well, I turned out fine." It's a comforting sentiment, often used to defend behaviors like yelling, over-disciplining, or ignoring emotional needs. But did we really turn out fine? Or have we simply adapted to dysfunction, carrying unresolved patterns into adulthood?

As a parent, I've said it myself—justifying tough moments with my children by leaning on my own upbringing. It wasn't until I started reflecting on my emotional scars that I realized how much I had normalized behaviors that had hurt me as a child. The truth is, acknowledging our struggles doesn't mean blaming our parents; it means being brave enough to break the cycle.

While writing this, I'm reminded of how I once felt it was too late to fix my adult kids—and in some ways, I was right. I can't go back and undo the mistakes I made, but I can acknowledge my toxic tendencies and be supportive of their healing journey. Most importantly, I've come to understand that while I felt I was doing my best at the time, I can't use that as a perpetual crutch to excuse areas where I needed growth. Sometimes, kids just need to hear us say, "I messed up," so they can let go of any self-blame they've carried, thinking they were the reason for our behavior.

The Unavoidable Reveal of Buried Hurt

Buried pain has a way of resurfacing when we least expect it, often in moments that seem unrelated to the original wound. This is because unresolved hurt doesn't simply vanish—it hides, waiting for triggers to bring it to the surface. The tricky part is that we often don't recognize these triggers for what they are. Instead, we find ourselves overreacting, feeling overwhelmed, or even lashing out without understanding why.

Example 1: The Unexpected Overreaction

Imagine you're running late to a meeting, and your child spills their drink on the floor. It's an accident—no harm intended—but you explode in anger. Later, you feel embarrassed and confused. Why such a big reaction to such a small mistake? When you dig deeper, you might discover it's not about the spilled drink at all. Maybe as a child, you were harshly criticized for making mistakes. That buried memory, paired with the stress of the moment, made your child's accident feel like a personal failure. Without even realizing it, your reaction wasn't to your child—it was to your past.

Example 2: The Quiet Pain of Perfectionism

You notice your teenager is struggling in school. Instead of offering support, you find yourself nagging them to "do better" or "work harder." Deep down, you might be projecting your own unresolved feelings of inadequacy—perhaps you were told as a child that you'd "never be good enough." Without addressing that pain, you unconsciously pass it on, creating the same pressure for your child that hurt you.

Example 3: Emotional Shutdown in Conflict

Think about a time when you had an argument with your spouse or co-parent, and instead of engaging, you completely shut down. Maybe you told yourself it wasn't worth the fight, but deep down, it's not about avoiding conflict. It's about a childhood where expressing feelings led to punishment or rejection. Your buried pain teaches you to equate conflict with danger, even in relationships that are supposed to feel safe. These moments, though painful, are opportunities. They shine a light on the hurt we've buried so deeply that we've stopped noticing its presence.

Recognizing Your "Yes, That's Me" Moment

Do you find yourself overly critical of your child's mistakes? This could stem from a childhood where your own mistakes were harshly punished.

Do you avoid difficult conversations with your kids or partner? This might point to a fear of conflict rooted in your past.

Do you feel anger or resentment bubbling up in situations that seem minor? Ask yourself if the intensity of your feelings matches the situation—or if you're reacting to something unresolved from your own childhood.

Parenting in Action

A father who grew up in a household where mistakes were met with harsh punishment repeated the same pattern with his own children. His son later admitted, "I didn't feel safe coming to you when I messed up. I was too afraid." The father realized he was parenting from his own fear of authority rather than creating a nurturing environment. This unconscious behavior often becomes second nature, unnoticed in the heat of parenting. However, moments of reflection can create a crucial pause—just enough time to acknowledge, "I can do better." These moments of self-awareness, though small, can have a profound impact on breaking cycles and fostering more intentional parenting.

The Parenting Parallel: Marketing's Hidden Messages

In marketing, we're often influenced by subconscious triggers—colors, music, or slogans that remind us of something familiar. These triggers tap into buried emotions to shape our decisions.

Parenting works the same way. Our buried pain serves as a trigger, guiding our actions in ways we don't always recognize.

For example, just as a jingle from your childhood might make you buy a certain cereal, a harsh word from your past might make you respond to your child's behavior in a way that surprises even you. Recognizing these patterns is the first step to rewriting them.

Your Next Step

Start keeping a journal of your emotional responses to parenting challenges. When you find yourself reacting strongly, take a moment to ask:

"What does this remind me of?"

"Am I reacting to the present situation, or is this tied to something from my past?"

"What can I do differently next time to respond with intention rather than reaction?"

Emotional Intelligence (EI) Insight: Breaking Authority Bias

Authority bias in parenting can prevent us from questioning our own habits. Emotional intelligence helps us approach these patterns with curiosity and compassion. By increasing self-awareness, we can identify which inherited behaviors serve our children and which ones need reimagining.

Self-Awareness: Recognize triggers that stem from buried hurt. The more you understand where your reactions come from, the more control you'll have over them.

Empathy: Consider how your child feels when faced with your overreaction. This helps create space for a softer, more intentional response.

Adaptability: Be open to experimenting with new approaches. Just like old wounds need time and care to heal, breaking cycles requires patience and flexibility.

Why It Matters

Unresolved pain isn't just about your past—it's about your child's future. By doing the work to confront and heal your own hurt, you're modeling emotional resilience and showing your child that it's okay to face their own struggles. You're also creating a healthier, more connected relationship that's built on understanding rather than unconscious reactions.

Reflection

Think of a moment when your reaction surprised even you. What might have been the underlying trigger?
How do you think your child interprets your reactions?

What steps can you take to pause, reflect, and respond differently next time?

Breaking the cycle starts with self-awareness. When you begin to unpack your own pain, you free yourself—and your child—from repeating it. This is how generational healing begins.

Chapter 3: The Power of the First Five Years

The first five years of a child's life are like wet cement—what we model and teach during this time leaves a lasting imprint. It's easy to overlook how these early experiences shape not only who our children become but how they process emotions, form relationships, and view themselves. Many of us think, "They're too young to remember this," but science shows otherwise.

Parenting in Action:

A mother shared with me during a coaching session that her toddler started apologizing excessively for minor mistakes. She realized that every time she got frustrated and sighed, her child internalized it as disappointment. The toddler had learned, unintentionally, to equate mistakes with failure.

As I reflect on my parenting journey, one moment that stands out vividly is my daughter not wanting to go into stores with me anymore. At first, I was confused because our shopping trips were something I treasured—a special time for just the two of us. I gave her whatever she wanted because I never wanted her to feel like she couldn't have it all. Another projection that we will discuss later in the book under the money chapter. It wasn't until I began therapy that I uncovered the real reason behind her reluctance. What I thought was girl time was actually causing her discomfort. When staff or others in the store frustrated me, or when I felt customer service didn't meet my expectations, I became very vocal. My tone was often harsh—though I'll admit, even now, I'm downplaying it a little out of embarrassment. But I promised myself that I'd be as real as possible in sharing my story, so here it is. I would go so far as to having to speak to a manager, voice my complaint and of course I felt I had to WIN.

My reactions, which I believed were justified, embarrassed her. Now that she's older, she's shared with me how these experiences shaped her—leaving her hesitant to speak up for herself for fear of sounding like me.

    Looking back, I realize I unconsciously missed an opportunity to model how to handle expectations and navigate the world with grace and like the Queen I am or was born to be. Instead, I modeled a form of "bullying" behavior, rooted in the belief I grew up with: "The customer is always right"—and the misguided notion that yelling would make people understand. And I'll admit—I felt justified in my actions at the time, but seeing how my daughter constantly struggles with speaking up for herself even when its really necessary really shows me how I hindered her ability to effectively communicate. It could be something as simple as asking for a discount or anything. She simply will avoid all conflict by any means necessary.

I constantly ask myself now how did I miss it, why couldn't I see it? Was being right worth it? The answer, as I look back, is no.

Those were valuable moments where I could have demonstrated emotional regulation, patience, and constructive communication—lessons that would have served her far better than my outbursts ever did.

The Parenting Parallel:

In marketing, the first impression of a brand sets the tone for its long-term reputation. Similarly, the foundational years of parenting shape a child's emotional framework. Just as a strong brand launch ensures loyalty, the consistency and love we show in the first five years creates emotional security that can last a lifetime and stand as a foundation when kids go through their adulting stage.

Key Elements to Focus On

Because Routines Matter: Regular bedtime stories, shared meals, collaborative conversations at any age, taking the time to role play how to effectively handle conflict and playtime establish trust and connection.

Here's another personal reflection that became clear as my son grew older. One day, he told me plainly: "You traumatized me when it came to reading." His words stung, but they also forced me to deeply reflect on my actions as a parent. I was so worried about him not reading well that I resorted to force and harsh punishments, like making him sit at the table for long periods or putting him on strict restrictions, thinking it would somehow motivate him.

In contrast, I took a completely different approach with my daughter. I introduced her to Barnes & Nobles at an early age, where she often saw me reading. By modeling a love for books and creating a routine centered around reading, she developed her own love for books, which she carries to this day. My son, on the other hand, avoids books at all costs—unless it's a comic book, which is where this reflection leads.

Looking back, I see how I mistakenly believed I could make him love reading through pressure and control. But instead of fostering a connection with books, I created resistance. I lacked emotional availability during this critical time, failing to meet him where he was emotionally. I didn't have the patience or the emotional intelligence to ask him why he didn't enjoy reading or what kinds of stories might interest him. Instead, I defaulted to the mindset of, "I'm the parent, and you'll do as I say."

Now, imagine the repeated message I sent to his developing mind: force and pressure are tools to make people do things. I unintentionally demonstrated that his feelings or preferences weren't as important as my expectations. Thankfully, he didn't adopt that behavior, but he also never developed a love for reading. Some might argue that maybe he just wasn't a "book person," but the truth is—I'll never know. My lack of emotional availability in those moments shaped his view of reading before he had the chance to form his own opinion.

Emotional Availability: Responding to your child's needs with empathy creates a secure attachment and an openness to allow them to grow.

Positive Reinforcement: Encouraging effort, not just outcomes, builds confidence and resilience.

Your Next Step:
Spend five minutes today focusing solely on your child—no phones, no distractions. Whether it's engaging in a game, reading a book, or simply listening to them talk, these moments are the ones they'll carry with them.

Reflect on This:
Think about your own early childhood. What memories stand out—good or bad? Were there small acts of love that made you feel seen? Or moments of neglect that left a lasting impact? How do those experiences influence how you show up as a parent today?

Emotional Intelligence (EI) Insight: Laying the Foundation Early

The first five years are critical for emotional development, and Emotional Intelligence is your greatest tool during this period. EI allows you to understand your own emotional triggers and manage them, creating a stable and nurturing environment for your child.

EI Applications for Early Years:
Self-Regulation: Learn to manage your stress so it doesn't spill over into interactions with your child. If they cry or throw a tantrum, take a moment to breathe before responding.
Empathy: See the world through your child's eyes. What might seem trivial to you—like wanting the "a specific" color cup—could feel monumental to them.
Intentional Communication: Narrate your actions and feelings. "Mommy is upset because she's tired, but it's not your fault" teaches children that emotions are normal and manageable.

Why EI Matters:

When parents model healthy emotional regulation and empathy during the early years, children develop secure attachments and emotional stability. These qualities will guide them through school, friendships, and eventually their own parenting journey.

Research Insight:

Research from Harvard's Center on the Developing Child shows that positive interactions during early childhood lay the groundwork for lifelong emotional health and resilience (Center on the Developing Child, n.d.).

Chapter 4: Yelling, Arguing, and Emotional Regulation

Yelling and arguing are often seen as unavoidable parts of parenting, especially when life feels overwhelming. But while venting frustrations may provide a temporary release for parents, it can feel like a personal attack to a child. Children interpret yelling as a threat, and repeated exposure can leave lasting emotional scars. This chapter explores the ripple effects of yelling and unresolved parental conflict on children's emotional health and offers strategies to break the cycle.

Parenting in Action:

I once worked with a teenager who shared, "Whenever my parents fought they would yell so loud, I would hide in my room and try to block out the noise. They told me it wasn't about me, but it always felt like my world was falling apart." Years later, she struggled to maintain relationships because she had internalized conflict as a sign of instability.

When the word **yelling** comes up, the first person that immediately comes to mind is my loving mother. I'm not sure if her mother yelled at her, but what I do know is that yelling was a foundational part of her parenting style. It wasn't just a tool; it was *the tool*, the definitive way to express authority in our household. As a child, I learned quickly—when Mom raised her voice, you didn't question, you obeyed.

Looking back, I realize yelling wasn't just about getting me to listen; it was a reflection of her own upbringing, her frustrations, and perhaps even her survival mechanisms. But as much as I loved and respected my mother, I can't deny that the yelling shaped me in ways that extended far beyond childhood obedience.

Yelling became my default setting as a parent, too. Without even realizing it, I had internalized her methods and passed them down to my own children. It wasn't intentional; in fact, I told myself I'd never be the kind of parent who yelled. But when life got overwhelming and I felt unheard, my voice would rise, and there I was—repeating the very pattern I swore to break.

Now, with the benefit of hindsight, I see that yelling did little to establish real authority. Instead, it most likely made me look like an adult who lacked the ability to articulate what I wanted to say with enough authority to command respect without raising my voice. Yelling might have made me seem powerful in the moment, but it also made me seem out of control—a soldier barking orders rather than a leader inspiring trust.

If my mom's goal was to raise a soldier, she absolutely succeeded. She taught me discipline, obedience, and the ability to endure. But if her goal was to raise an emotionally secure young woman—someone who could command authority with calm confidence, someone who didn't feel the need to yell to be heard—then, unfortunately, she missed the bar.

I don't say this to blame my mother; I say it to acknowledge the cycle. She did the best she could with the tools she had, and I know her love for me was never in question. But love and emotional security don't always go hand in hand. This realization has been one of the most humbling lessons of my parenting journey.

Marketing Parallel: The Cost of Negative Branding

In marketing, yelling could be reflected in a brand that uses aggressive, fear-based advertising to grab attention. It works temporarily but leaves a negative impression, eroding trust over time. A brand that constantly shouts at its audience risks alienating them, much like a parent who yells risks creating emotional distance.

Successful brands connect through clear, consistent, and emotionally resonant messaging. As parents, we can learn from this approach by replacing yelling with intentional, empathetic communication. A brand that listens and adapts builds loyalty; a parent who listens and adjusts builds trust.

Actionable Parenting Strategies: Breaking the Cycle

If yelling has been part of your parenting journey, it's never too late to break the cycle. Here are some actionable strategies to help you transform your communication and create a more emotionally secure environment for your children:

Pause and Reflect

Before reacting, take a moment to pause and identify your emotions. Are you yelling out of frustration, fear, or exhaustion? Recognizing your triggers can help you respond thoughtfully instead of reacting impulsively.

Try This: When you feel the urge to yell, take three deep breaths and count to five. If needed, step away for a moment to collect your thoughts.

Reframe Authority

Authority doesn't have to be loud. True authority comes from consistency, empathy, and clarity. Instead of shouting to be heard, focus on connecting with your child's perspective.

Try This: Use "I" statements to express your needs calmly. For example, "I feel upset when the rules aren't followed because it's important for us to work together."

Model Emotional Regulation

Children learn how to handle emotions by watching us. By managing your frustration calmly, you show them how to navigate their own big feelings.

Try This: Share your process aloud. "I'm feeling really frustrated right now, so I'm going to take a moment to calm down before we talk."

Repair When Necessary

If you do yell, acknowledge it and repair the moment. Apologizing doesn't weaken your authority; it strengthens trust.

Try This: Say, "I'm sorry for yelling earlier. I was upset, but I should have spoken to you calmly. Let's talk about it now."

Create a Family Communication Plan

Set expectations for how conflicts will be handled in your home. Create a plan together as a family, emphasizing calm problem-solving over reactive responses.

Try This: Hold a family meeting to discuss communication goals, such as using kind words, active listening, and taking breaks during conflicts.

Your Next Step:

This week, commit to identifying one yelling trigger and replacing it with a calm, intentional response. Write down how it felt for both you and your child and celebrate the small step towards breaking the cycle.

Reflect on This:

If yelling were a marketing campaign, what message would it send to your child? Is it the message you want to communicate, or is it time for a rebrand?

Final Thought:

Breaking the cycle of yelling isn't easy, but it's one of the most impactful changes you can make as a parent. By replacing yelling with empathy and intentionality, you're not just creating a healthier home—you're giving your child the tools to thrive emotionally, now and in the future.

The Parenting Parallel:

Think of yelling as negative PR for your family. It might grab attention in the moment, but over time, it erodes trust and damages relationships. On the other hand, calm and intentional communication acts like positive reinforcement, building stronger bonds and healthier patterns. Just as marketing thrives on trust, so does effective parenting.

Key Strategies for Breaking the Cycle

The Impact of Yelling: Children raised in environments where yelling is frequent are more likely to develop anxiety and struggle with emotional regulation.

Arguments and Emotional Safety: Unresolved parental conflict creates insecurity in children, who may blame themselves for the tension.

Teaching by Example: Modeling calm responses helps children develop their own emotional regulation skills.

Your Next Step:

The next time you feel the urge to yell, take three deep breaths and pause before responding. Practice using "I" statements to express your feelings calmly. For example, say, "I feel overwhelmed right now and need a moment to think."

Reflect on This:

When was the last time you yelled or argued in front of your child? How do you think they interpreted the situation? What can you do differently next time to model healthier conflict resolution?

Emotional Intelligence (EI) Insight: Modeling Emotional Regulation and Turning Frustration Into Growth

Emotional intelligence allows parents to manage their own stress and model effective conflict resolution. With EI, you can recognize when frustration is building, regulate your emotions, and approach situations with empathy, setting the tone for how your child will handle conflict in their own life.

EI Applications for Conflict Resolution:

Self-Awareness: Identify your emotional triggers and patterns. Are you reacting from stress, fear, or frustration? Recognize when stress is building and pause before reacting.

Self-Regulation: Practice calming techniques like deep breathing or stepping away for a moment to gather your thoughts.

Empathy: Consider how your child feels when they witness yelling or arguments. Are they scared, confused, or hurt? Validate their emotions and provide comfort.

Adaptability: Practice new ways of responding, even if it feels uncomfortable at first.

Why EI Matters:

When children see parents managing emotions effectively, they learn to do the same. This builds emotional resilience and helps them navigate conflicts with peers, teachers, and eventually their own families. When parents develop emotional intelligence, they create a home environment where children feel safe, respected, and valued. This fosters emotional resilience, trust, and stronger relationships.

Research Insight:

Studies from the American Psychological Association (APA) emphasize that children exposed to frequent yelling are more likely to struggle with anxiety and develop similar conflict styles in adulthood. Positive conflict resolution modeling can mitigate these effects (APA, 2018).

Chapter 5: My Achilles Heel: Money, Spending, and the Mask of Insecurity

This chapter, more than any other, is my Achilles heel—a deeply personal struggle that has impacted my life in the past, the present, and, I hope, not my future. For years, I wrestled with bad spending habits and obsessive shopping sprees that ultimately buried me in credit card debt and left me overwhelmed by an overabundance of items I didn't need, lawsuits and just pure embarrassment. Working with my psychologist was the first time I truly confronted and began to understand the "whys" behind these episodes. Almost like a gambler or someone addicted to something else, compulsive spending was my poison.

The hardest part of this journey? I was supposed to be the financial guru. I was the one giving advice, creating budgets, and empowering others to achieve financial freedom. I knew better, but I couldn't do better. That dichotomy—being someone who inspired others while feeling like a fraud inside—was devastating. Deep down, I was stuck in a cycle of shame and self-doubt, unable to reconcile the gap between what I taught and how I lived.

This struggle didn't just impact me; it rippled out and created stress in my home environment. On the surface, I tried to project confidence and control, but underneath, I was drowning in anxiety and guilt. The breaking point came during COVID when our household income drastically changed. The financial strain brought my spending habits to light in a way I could no longer ignore or justify. My compulsive shopping wasn't just about acquiring things; it was about masking my insecurities and soothing emotions I didn't know how to process. And it wasn't just my struggle—it was impacting my children, too.

My daughter was old enough to notice the patterns. She saw me buy makeup, clothes, and other items I didn't need, all while I tried to mask my own feelings of inadequacy. Whether I was conscious of it or not, I was teaching her something about money—not through my words, but through my actions. I was showing her that spending could be used as a coping mechanism, that material things could temporarily fill emotional voids. This is the essence of what this book is about: children internalize the behaviors they observe, not just the lessons we try to teach them directly.

Over time, I began to notice the subtle ways my habits influenced her relationship with money. My spending habits had unknowingly become my kids blueprint and my husband in my mind secretly blamed me or at least that's what I had internalized in my own head. My obsessive episodes were directly contributing to my stress and instability. Both of my children were shaping their financial values based on the unspoken lessons I was modeling, and neither was healthy.

The Lesson in Reflection

When I started therapy, I had to face the hard truth: my spending wasn't just about wanting more things. It was about covering up insecurities, trying to prove something to myself, or finding momentary relief from stress. But in doing so, I sent a message to my children that was far from empowering. I showed them that money wasn't a tool for stability, growth, or joy—it was a means of escape or a source of shame.

This realization forced me to reflect on how these behaviors tied into the larger themes of this book. Just as children absorb the emotional environment around them, they also absorb the financial atmosphere we create. If money is a source of tension, avoidance, or overindulgence, they internalize those lessons. They don't learn how to manage money effectively; they learn how to react to it emotionally, often in ways that mirror our own unresolved issues.

The Ripple Effects on My Spouse and Family

As much as my spending habits affected me and my children, the person who bore the brunt of this stress was my spouse. My financial choices created constant tension in our marriage, with arguments often sparked by my inability to stay within a budget or live below my means. Our kids would witness these fights, absorbing the financial anxiety and confusion that hung like a cloud over our household. Instead of feeling secure and stable, they saw financial stress as a norm, even though we technically made enough money to live comfortably. The problem wasn't our income—it was my inability to face the reality of my overspending.

My husband, time and time again, stepped in to bail me out—whether it was paying off credit card debt or finding ways to cover the financial gaps my spending created. But like any addiction, I would find myself right back in the same cycle of bad decisions, leaving him to worry constantly about the state of our finances. It was a painful reality to watch him shoulder the burden of my choices, knowing that he deserved better. His unwavering support and patience were remarkable, but I know it came at a cost to his own peace of mind.

Even now, I'm still working through this. There are no quick fixes, and the road to recovery is ongoing. I wish there was more focus and resources dedicated to helping people like me—those who know better but struggle to break free from the emotional and psychological grip of overspending. I know I'm not alone in this, and it's a reality that many families face in silence. Financial struggles aren't always about numbers on a spreadsheet; they're deeply tied to emotional wounds, societal pressures, and personal insecurities.

For anyone reading this who resonates with my story, know that I'm standing on the hopes that change is possible. It starts with acknowledging the problem and seeking help—not just for yourself, but for the people who love you and deserve to see you at your best. This chapter isn't just a reflection of my mistakes; it's a call for compassion, understanding, and support for those navigating this all-too-common battle.

Money is one of those things we think we can shield our kids from, but the truth is, they feel its weight. And when you come from nothing one of the worst mistakes we do as parents is trying to give our kids everything by any means necessary. This mindset causes whispered arguments about bills or creates visible strains of making ends meet, and our children pick up on far more than we realize. Even when we don't explicitly involve them in financial discussions, they absorb the emotional atmosphere surrounding money.

The Bigger Picture

Whether it's yelling, arguing, or in this case, spending, our behaviors continue to create this blueprint for how our children will navigate the world. My story is a reminder that even when we feel like we've failed, there's always room to course-correct.

The message I want to leave you with is this: it's never too late to change the narrative. By recognizing our own struggles and taking steps to heal, we not only transform ourselves but also give our children the tools to build healthier, more intentional lives. Financial wellness, like emotional wellness, starts with awareness.

And the earlier we start modeling the behaviors we want to see, the stronger the foundation we lay for their future.

A Commitment to Change

Breaking this cycle isn't easy, but I have started with small steps. First, I had to be honest with my children and let them know that my need to give them everything was not from a good place. It was a place of filling my own internal void as to where I thought I could make them happy. I acknowledged my mistakes, explained why I was working to change, and made a commitment to do better—not just for myself but for them. I began involving them in financial conversations and for the first time telling them "No" something I rarely did in fear of them thinking we were poor. I'm personally more open to talking about budgets and saving, but also about the emotional side of money—how to recognize when spending becomes a crutch and how to build a healthy relationship with it.

I also had to model healthier behaviors. Instead of buying makeup or clothes to fill a void, I focused on creating moments of connection—sharing a meal, going for a walk, coloring, or having conversations that didn't involve spending. I also had to separate myself from friends and social media that would remind me of impulse spending. I wanted my children to see that happiness and self-worth come from within, not from what we buy.

Parenting in Action:

I remember now as I reflect back on both of my kids starting to say, "It's okay, I don't need anything." My children had overheard arguments about finances and internalized the idea that their needs were a burden. This unspoken stress shaped their relationship with money for years to come. I'm hoping that I can at least bring normalcy to an area that I kept hidden in hopes of breaking this financial generational burden.

The Parenting Parallel:

In marketing, money and value perception are key drivers of consumer behavior. Similarly, children learn to perceive money—and their worth—through the way we handle finances. Just as brands aim to create positive value associations, and scarcity tactics parents can intentionally shape their children's understanding of money in empowering ways.

Shaping Healthy Financial Messages for Kids
Open Conversations:

Instead of avoiding the topic, discuss money in age-appropriate ways. This normalizes financial literacy and removes the mystery and fear around finances.

Modeling Problem-Solving:

When financial challenges arise, involve your child in simple, constructive ways—like choosing between two grocery items. This shows them how to navigate limitations without fear. Last but not least this is the perfect time to start showing your kids the power of delayed gratification. This was a mindset that was so hard for me personally because I felt if I wanted something I had the right to get it right away. I didn't budget for it, I didn't think twice about it. All I would check is if I had the money then I was able to have it.

Creating Positive Associations:

Highlight how money can be used for good—saving, sharing, and achieving goals—rather than only focusing on scarcity or fear.

Your Next Step:

Start a simple financial activity with your child, like saving coins in a jar for a family treat. Explain how small steps add up to big goals, creating a positive connection with money.

Reflect on This:

What are your children learning from how you handle money? Are you teaching them confidence and problem-solving, or are they absorbing anxiety and fear? Reflect on the messages you may have unintentionally sent and consider how you might shift them.

Emotional Intelligence (EI) Insight: Managing Financial Stress

Emotional Intelligence helps parents regulate their own financial anxieties, ensuring those emotions don't spill over onto their children. By approaching money with calm and transparency, parents can model a healthier relationship with finances.

EI Applications for Financial Conversations:
Self-Regulation:

Recognize when financial stress is influencing your mood or interactions. Take a moment to ground yourself before discussing money in front of your child.

Empathy:

Consider how financial discussions might feel to your child. Reassure them that financial challenges are temporary and not their responsibility.

Intentional Communication:

Use clear, age-appropriate language to explain financial decisions without creating fear.

Why EI Matters:

When parents model calm and constructive approaches to finances, children develop resilience and problem-solving skills. This prepares them to navigate their own financial journeys with confidence rather than fear.

Research Insight:

The Brookings Institution emphasizes that early financial education and open family discussions about money contribute to healthier financial habits and greater resilience in adulthood.

Chapter 6: The Role of Grandparents and Extended Family

Parenting doesn't happen in a vacuum. Grandparents, aunts, uncles, and other extended family members often play significant roles in shaping a child's values, beliefs, and behaviors. Whether through direct interactions or simply observing their behavior, children absorb messages from their wider family network.

Extended Family Influence: Secondary "Marketers" of Beliefs

This chapter examines how extended family acts as secondary "marketers" of beliefs and how their influence can either reinforce or challenge parental messaging.
I once spoke with a teenager who said, "Every time I look in the mirror, I hear my cousin's voice telling me I need to lose weight." Despite her parents' genuine efforts to build her confidence and promote a positive body image, the critical comments from her cousin overshadowed their attempts. Her parents' praise became muffled under the weight of those repeated words, which etched themselves into her mind, shaping her self-esteem in ways her parents could never have anticipated.

To be perfectly honest, we can't always control what others say, especially family members, and some of you may hold the belief that "words don't hurt." But I'm here to remind you that words do hurt. Words can empower, break down, or cause one to spiral into self-doubt. This is precisely why family conversations must revolve around reinforcing the values of your household.

If extended family members can't honor those values, it's your responsibility to set boundaries—even if that means limiting exposure to environments that don't align with the positive reinforcement you're striving to build. This isn't about cutting ties unnecessarily; it's about protecting the emotional health of your family.

For this teenager, her cousin's thoughtless remarks became a subconscious script, one that continuously played in her mind every time she saw her reflection. These words, simple to some but powerful to her, left a lasting imprint that undermined her parents' efforts and caused deep, long-term insecurities. What she shared with me serves as a powerful reminder: even well-meaning family members can unintentionally damage a child's sense of self-worth through careless or repetitive remarks.

It underscores the importance of being intentional about the narratives we expose our children to and ensuring those narratives align with the emotional and psychological values we're working hard to instill.

As parents, it's critical to engage in ongoing reflection and open conversations with extended family. Let them know the values you're instilling in your children and ask them to help reinforce those values rather than unknowingly counteract them. In some cases, this might mean gently correcting someone or standing firm in your decision to create boundaries for the sake of your child's well-being.

Ultimately, the goal isn't to create conflict but to protect the emotional ecosystem you're nurturing for your family. Because at the end of the day, the words children internalize—whether from parents, cousins, or other relatives—have a direct or indirect impact that will shape their sense of identity, self-worth, and resilience because repetition/reinforcement is at play. It's up to us to make sure those words are uplifting, not undermining.

The Power of Words: Protecting Our Children from Harmful Narratives

I vividly remember a specific family member who would make comments about my son's complexion. Each time, I would immediately respond, often angrily, only for the remarks to be dismissed as "harmless" or "just a joke." But let me be crystal clear: there is nothing harmless about thoughtless comments or ignorant questions that chip away at a child's sense of identity and self-worth.

If you take nothing else from this book, let it be this: if you don't have anything nice to say, keep your mouth shut. If you're tempted to ask a question that borders on ignorance or insensitivity, ask yourself first, "Is this necessary? Is it kind? Is it respectful?" Stop being bold for the wrong reasons.
Relatives might say things like, "You better not end up like your mom, running around with boys," or "Don't grow up to be a dealer like your dad." These comments, often masked as warnings, are harmful projections rooted in fear and judgment rather than encouragement. Instead of guiding children toward a positive future, such remarks anchor them to their parents' past struggles, unfairly assigning them a narrative they didn't choose. These words don't protect—they plant seeds of doubt, shame, and defiance, often steering children toward the very behaviors the family fears. It's a harsh reminder that projecting one's anxieties onto a child can harm their sense of identity and potential. We must replace these damaging projections with affirmations that inspire children to see their unique value and capabilities, free from the shadows of the past.

The irony is that many of the people who feel emboldened to make these comments are often the same ones who struggle to advocate for themselves in meaningful ways. They shy away from standing up for themselves at work, avoid public speaking, and secretly battle deep insecurities of their own.

Instead of addressing those flaws, they project them outward in the form of what they call "harmless banter."

I'll admit, even as I write this, I feel the sting of those moments. It's a reminder of how words can cut deeply, especially when we're trying so hard as parents to build our children up. I've spent countless hours pouring love and affirmations into my son, reminding him how unique and handsome he is. Yet, when family members and even close friends—those who should serve as an extension of his safe space—make ignorant comments, it threatens to undo those efforts in an instant.

My son has a lighter complexion, and the comments ranged from questions about whether he was albino to suggestions that he "looked white." Let me say this: there is absolutely nothing wrong with albinism, and every skin tone is beautiful, just as God made us. However, these questions weren't rooted in curiosity or kindness; they were a reflection of ignorance and insensitivity. "It's similar to asking a Black person if they're White, or the reverse." It just isn't a polite question at all. These kinds of questions don't just showcase a lack of education; they send a message to children that making such remarks is acceptable behavior.

When kids hear adults speak without thought or respect, they internalize those behaviors as normal. They might carry that same insensitivity into the world, perpetuating cycles of ignorance and harm. This is why what our children see and hear—especially from the people closest to them—sets the tone for what they replicate in their own lives.

Creating Safe Spaces: How to Address these Difficult Conversations

As parents, it's exhausting to pour every ounce of energy into building our children's confidence, only to have it threatened by the thoughtlessness of others. But instead of retreating or avoiding these situations, we must address them head-on at times. Here's how you can start navigating these difficult conversations:

Call It Out Privately:

If a family member makes an insensitive comment, pull them aside privately. Let them know how their words impact your child and why they're harmful. For example, you might say: "I know you didn't mean any harm, but when you comment on [my child's complexion/appearance], it sends a message that there's something wrong with them. We're teaching [child's name] to love themselves as they are, and I'd appreciate it if you'd help reinforce that."

Set Expectations Before Gatherings:

If you anticipate problematic comments, have a conversation with key family members before the event. Say something like:

"We're working hard to build a positive environment for [child's name]. I'd really appreciate it if everyone could be mindful of their words. We want our family to be a place of love and encouragement."

Involve Allies:

Enlist the support of other family members who understand your values. Having others back you up can help reinforce the message and create a united front.

Model Appropriate Behavior:

When your child witnesses you are addressing these situations calmly and assertively, they learn how to handle similar scenarios. For instance, if someone makes an ignorant remark, respond with:

"Actually, [child's name] is perfect just as they are, and we don't focus on things like that in our family. Let's change the subject."

The Ripple Effect of Words

These efforts aren't just about protecting your child in the moment—they're about shaping the kind of environment you want them to thrive in. By addressing harmful behaviors within your family, you're teaching your child to value themselves and others. It's also a reminder to extended family members that their words carry weight. If we let these moments slide, we send a message that it's okay to say whatever comes to mind without considering the consequences. But by speaking up, we create accountability and set a higher standard for how we treat one another.

At the heart of it, this isn't just about my son or your child. It's about building a culture of respect, kindness, and understanding within our families. It's about ensuring that the love and empowerment we pour into our children aren't undone by careless words. And it's about reminding everyone in our circle that family should be a safe haven—not a source of insecurity or hurt. The work may be difficult, but it's worth it. Because when we create safe spaces for our children, we give them the foundation they need to carry confidence, resilience, and kindness into every corner of their lives.

The Parenting Parallel:

Think of extended family members as "influencers" in a marketing campaign. Just as influencers can shape consumer perceptions through their authority and reach, family members can amplify or conflict with the messages parents are trying to convey. The key is to ensure the "campaign" remains consistent, so children aren't receiving conflicting values.

Balancing Influence and Maintaining Consistency

The Power of Words: Offhand comments from extended family, like critiques about appearance or ability, can unintentionally undermine a child's confidence.

Aligning Messages: Discussing values and boundaries with extended family helps create a united front in raising children.

Balancing Influence: Encouraging positive contributions while addressing harmful patterns allows children to benefit from a diverse support network without confusion.

Your Next Step:

Start an open conversation with key family members about the values and behaviors you want to reinforce in your child. Be clear and empathetic in setting boundaries if needed, and express appreciation for their positive influence.

Reflect on This:

What messages are your children hearing from extended family members? Are these messages aligned with the values you want to instill? How can you strengthen the positive influences while addressing the negative ones?

Emotional Intelligence (EI) Insight: Navigating Family Dynamics

EI helps parents navigate the complex dynamics of extended family influence. By practicing empathy and effective communication, parents can address conflicting messages and maintain consistency in their child's environment.

EI Applications for Managing Extended Family Influence:

Empathy: Understand that family members often mean well, even when their actions or words conflict with your values.

Communication: Approach sensitive topics with clarity and kindness, ensuring that family members feel respected while addressing your concerns.

Boundary-Setting: Practice assertiveness to protect your child from negative messaging without alienating the family member involved.

Why EI Matters:

When parents use Emotional Intelligence to manage extended family dynamics, they create a stable and supportive environment for their children. This ensures that the child's emotional growth is nurtured, even within a diverse family network.

Research Insight:

Research from the Journal of Child and Family Studies highlights that children exposed to consistent, positive reinforcement from multiple caregivers are more likely to develop secure attachments and higher self-esteem. Conversely, mixed messaging can lead to confusion and insecurity.

Chapter 7: Single Parenting – Building Bridges, Not Walls

Single parenting is definitely not an easy task, whether you're a mom, dad, grandparent, aunt, or any other family member stepping into the role. The weight of being the sole provider, nurturer, and disciplinarian can feel overwhelming, and the emotional toll is often compounded by the absence of the other parent. Yet, one critical area that requires intentional effort is how we talk about the absent parent in front of the child.

Yes, I understand the frustration. It's natural to feel angry or hurt when you're carrying the brunt of parenting responsibilities while feeling the other parent isn't equally contributing. But as adults, we have to recognize that our words and actions hold immense power. You can either build a bridge for your child to navigate their relationship with the absent parent, or you can widen a gap that may take years to repair.

Let's address what I call the "bitter mom syndrome." This is when a mother uses the child as a pawn to punish the father because their romantic relationship didn't work out. It manifests in actions like withholding visits, bad-mouthing the father in front of the child, or making the child feel guilty for wanting to spend time with him. To those moms, I say this bluntly: **grow the hell up.** Relationships end. People lose feelings. But none of that should interfere with ensuring your child doesn't unconsciously feel they're the source of all this anger, hurt, and pain.

Here's where the marketing parallel comes in: brands exit relationships all the time. Think of a company that ends a sponsorship or a partnership. They may no longer work together, but they remain professional because their shared audience (in this case, your child) is still watching. Successful brands know that airing grievances publicly can tarnish their reputation. Similarly, as parents, we have to maintain a level of grace, not for the other parent's sake, but for the child who sees and hears everything.

Now let's shift focus to the absent fathers—or as I call them, the "deadbeat dads." Some men think that if they're sending money, they've fulfilled their obligations. But parenting isn't just about financial support. It's about being present, emotionally and physically, and showing your child that they matter. If you're prioritizing your ego, your new relationship, or your career over your child, you're failing them in ways money can't fix.

Get it the hell together. Your child didn't ask to be here. They didn't ask for a parent who half-shows up. If you're a father who thinks a paycheck is enough while your child goes without your time, attention, and love, then you are doing them a disservice they will carry for life.

When fathers take this detached approach, children often feel abandoned or rejected. They see their mother struggling to make ends meet, working long hours, and sacrificing her own needs just to ensure they have what they need. This creates internal resentment. Children may grow up feeling, "Why didn't my dad care enough to help?" or, "Why was I not important enough for him to stick around?" These feelings of rejection can manifest as anger, difficulty trusting others, or even mimicking the same behavior in their own relationships later in life.

The Illusion of Equality: Lessons from Brand Placement

Parenting and co-parenting aren't the only arenas where the concept of equality often misses the mark. Consider the world of marketing and retail. Every brand aspires to be treated equally, with premium shelf space, prominent advertisements, and favorable positioning in stores. But the reality is far different.

Not all brands are created equal in the eyes of retailers, and there are countless factors that determine why one product ends up front and center while another is relegated to the bottom shelf. Factors like profit margins, consumer demand, relationships with distributors, and brand recognition all play a role.
Does this mean the brand on the bottom shelf is less valuable? Not necessarily. It just means the circumstances didn't align for equal placement—and that's okay. Similarly, when families separate or co-parent, external forces like court systems, financial

stability, or logistical arrangements set the circumstances. Judges, mediators, and even societal norms often play a role in defining what parenting arrangements look like, and those decisions might not always feel "equal" to one or both parents. But like in retail, equality isn't the goal—the goal is effectiveness and collaboration for the sake of the child.

Prioritize the End Goal, Not Equal Placement

In retail, successful brands focus less on whether they're placed on the top shelf or the bottom shelf and more on how they connect with consumers. Similarly, in co-parenting, the focus shouldn't be on achieving an exact balance of tasks or time, but on ensuring that the child feels supported, loved, and secure. It's not about who spends more time or who contributes more money. It's about showing up, being consistent, and building a united front, even when circumstances aren't perfectly "equal."

When external forces like courts or mediators determine parenting plans, it's easy to feel like the outcome is unfair or tilted. But just as brands find ways to thrive regardless of placement, parents have to focus on what they can control—showing up for their child, making the most of their time, and ensuring their presence adds value to the child's life.

A Marketing Mindset for Parenting

Retail brands know that placement isn't the only factor in their success. They invest in other strategies, like engaging packaging, memorable ads, and strong customer relationships. As parents, we can take a similar approach. Maybe one parent handles more day-to-day responsibilities while the other focuses on quality time during visits. Maybe one contributes more financially while the other provides emotional support. The key is recognizing that it's not about being equal—it's about being effective.

It's about acknowledging that circumstances might not always feel fair or balanced, but what truly matters is that your child feels like they have two parents working toward their success. By focusing on collaboration rather than competition, you create a narrative of support and teamwork that your child can carry with them into their own future relationships.

The Power of Perspective

At the end of the day, the circumstances set by external forces, like judges or societal norms, are just a starting point. What you do within those circumstances defines the outcome. Focus less on fairness and more on what will help your child thrive. Just like successful brands prioritize building trust with consumers, successful co-parents prioritize building a united front for the sake of their children. When the focus is on your child, everyone wins.

The Ripple Effect

The absence of a parent—or the toxic dynamic created when one parent bad-mouths the other—doesn't just impact a child's view of their parents. It shapes their worldview. Just like in marketing, where a brand's narrative influences how consumers perceive them, the "narrative" children grow up hearing about their family dynamics shapes their sense of self and relationships. Here are some examples of how children experience these situations:

Mimicking unhealthy relationships: If a child consistently hears one parent speaking negatively about the other, they may grow up thinking it's normal to tear down people they're upset with, rather than communicate or resolve conflict.

Emotional detachment: Children who feel caught in the crossfire of their parents' conflict may learn to shut down emotionally as a defense mechanism. This can impact their ability to form deep, trusting relationships in adulthood.

Identity struggles: When one parent is absent or painted in a negative light, children may struggle with understanding their own identity, especially if they see traits of the absent parent in themselves.

Role reversal: In some cases, children may feel the need to "parent" their own parent—comforting their mom when she cries or stepping in to take on responsibilities that aren't theirs to bear. This forces them to grow up too quickly and robs them of their childhood.

Starting Difficult Conversations

So, how do we break this cycle? How do we ensure that single parenting doesn't leave a legacy of resentment, confusion, or broken relationships? It starts with difficult but necessary conversations:

Call out harmful behavior: If you have a family member or friend who regularly speaks negatively about your child's other parent in front of your child, address it directly. Pull them aside and say, "I know you're trying to be supportive, but it's important to me that we don't talk about [their dad/mom] like that in front of them. They need to form their own opinions, not absorb our frustrations."

Set boundaries before family gatherings: If you know certain relatives have a habit of making harmful comments, address it proactively. Before a family event, have a private conversation with that person: "I need to ask for your help in creating a positive environment for [child's name]. Please avoid bringing up anything negative about [the other parent] while we're together. It's really important for their emotional well-being."

Be honest with your child—at their level: If your child asks difficult questions about the absent parent, answer them with honesty, but without bitterness. For example, you might say, "Your dad isn't able to be here as much as I'd like, but that's not your fault. He loves you in his own way, and I'll always be here to make sure you have what you need."

Seek support for yourself: Single parenting is tough, and it's okay to feel frustrated, overwhelmed, or even angry. But those emotions shouldn't spill onto your child. Consider therapy, support groups, or talking to a trusted friend to process your feelings and find healthier ways to cope.

Moving Forward

Single parenting is an opportunity to show your child resilience, strength, and unconditional love. It's not about being perfect; it's about being intentional. By being mindful of your words and actions, setting boundaries with others, and prioritizing your child's emotional well-being, you can create a safe, loving environment where they can thrive—even in the absence of the other parent.

Remember, your child is watching and learning. The "brand" you're building in your family is one they will carry forward into their own relationships. Just like a strong marketing message, consistency, positivity, and authenticity matter. Be the bridge that connects them to a healthy, stable future—not the wall that divides them from it.

The Parenting Parallel:

Single parents are like personal brands in the world of parenting—they market strength, adaptability, and perseverance. Just as a brand conveys its core values through consistent messaging, single parents communicate resilience through their actions and attitudes. Children absorb these values by watching how their parent handles challenges, making resilience a core part of their "family brand."

Building Resilience as a Single Parent

Emotional Availability: Being emotionally present for your child creates a sense of security that outweighs material resources.

Resilience by Example: Demonstrating perseverance in the face of challenges teaches children to adapt and thrive.

The Importance of Self-Care: Prioritizing your well-being benefits both you and your child by reducing stress and modeling healthy habits.

Your Next Step:

Choose one small act of self-care you can commit to this week, whether it's taking a walk, journaling, or enjoying a quiet cup of coffee. Share a story with your child about a time when you overcame a challenge and invite them to share their own stories of resilience.

Reflect on This:

Are you focusing on what you can provide emotionally, or are you overly concerned about what's missing? What messages is your child absorbing from the way you handle challenges?

Emotional Intelligence (EI) Insight: Navigating Single Parenthood

EI is a crucial tool for single parents, helping them manage stress, build strong connections with their children, and maintain a sense of balance. Self-awareness allows single parents to recognize their emotional needs, while empathy helps them understand and support their child's unique experiences.

EI Applications for Single Parenting:

Self-Awareness: Recognize when you're running on empty and need to recharge. Acknowledge your limits without guilt.

Empathy: Understand your child's perspective and validate their feelings, especially when they express frustrations or fears.

Intentional Communication: Use positive language to frame challenges as opportunities for growth and connection.

Why EI Matters:

When single parents model emotional intelligence, they teach their children how to navigate challenges with grace and self-assurance. This creates a foundation for lifelong emotional resilience.

Research Insight:

Research from the American Academy of Pediatrics highlights that children in single-parent households thrive when they experience consistent emotional support and structure. Self-care for parents is also shown to reduce stress and improve parenting outcomes.

Chapter 8: Projections and the Weight of the Past

We often think we're parenting in the moment, but in truth, much of our behavior as parents is shaped by our own past. Unresolved childhood trauma, unmet expectations, or lingering fears can seep into our parenting, manifesting as overprotectiveness, perfectionism, or projecting our dreams and insecurities onto our children.

Boy did my husband and I stumble in this part of parenting. Maybe "screw up" is too harsh, but if I could go back, I'd love to have had a book like this to help me realize that our children are not characters we create—they are individuals meant to grow into the people they are intended to be. Our job isn't to write their story; it's to support them as they write their own.

It's hard for me to admit, but as someone who has struggled with self-worth, self-sabotaging tendencies, and a poor relationship with money, I now know there is no career, no amount of money, and no societal checklist that guarantees happiness. True joy comes from the foundation we build within ourselves—the ability to apply emotional intelligence, embrace resilience, and bloom into the person we feel most comfortable being.

Parenting from Fear, Not Empowerment

Unfortunately, many of us parent from a place of fear rather than empowerment. We try to shield our children from the mistakes and failures we endured. In doing so, we unintentionally project our own fears, traumas, and unfulfilled dreams onto them. We act as though we are the authors of their stories, crafting characters with no flaws—particularly flaws that remind us of ourselves. But when we parent this way, we don't empower our children to succeed; we burden them with the weight of our own insecurities.

I've come to realize that this mindset, no matter how well-intentioned, creates tension in the parent-child dynamic. Even parents with wealth and privilege fall into this trap, leading to a generation of kids who may have every opportunity but still feel miserable, disconnected, or lost. Why? Because success isn't rooted in external achievements; it's built on internal emotional stability.

And let's address the common refrain: "There's no book for parenting." While it's true there's no definitive manual, there are plenty of books and resources available to help us see parenting from different perspectives. The real issue isn't the lack of guidance—it's our lack of discipline as parents to be lifelong learners and adapt as the world changes.

Working on Myself Before Parenting

If I could do it all over again, I would have worked on myself emotionally before bringing kids into the world. Not because I think I could have been a perfect parent (that doesn't exist), but because I could have been an empowered parent. I could have modeled behaviors rooted in self-awareness rather than reactionary fear.

Here's the harsh reality: God doesn't make mistakes. I believe I went through these storms with my own kids so I could write this book and, hopefully, help others stop using the excuse, "There's no book for parenting." The truth is, there are books—and we just need to be willing to read, reflect, and grow.

Projecting My Past onto My Kids

Reflecting on my own journey, I can see how I projected my unresolved fears onto my children. With my daughter, I unintentionally passed down my fear of not being successful. Because I struggled with my own self-worth, I imposed expectations on her to overachieve, fearing she might face the same insecurities I had. Instead of empowering her to define success on her own terms, I created a narrative rooted in my fear of failure.

With my son, I projected the pain of being hurt by men in my own life. I enforced a strict code of behavior, insisting he always be good to women. While teaching respect and kindness are valuable lessons, the foundation shouldn't have been rooted in my past traumas. Instead of guiding him to be a good person for his own growth and relationships, I inadvertently tied his identity to avoiding my own pain.

These projections may not seem harmful on the surface, but they created an undercurrent of expectation. My children weren't being taught to thrive—they were being taught to compensate for my unresolved wounds.

The Marketing Parallel: Crafting Authentic Campaigns

Let's bring this into the world of marketing. Imagine a brand that's trying to appeal to its audience but is operating from fear—fear of competition, fear of rejection, or fear of losing relevance. That brand's messaging becomes reactive, inauthentic, and disconnected. Instead of resonating with its audience, it creates confusion and distrust.

The same applies to parenting. When we project our fears onto our children, we aren't crafting authentic messages. Instead, we're creating a narrative that doesn't align with their individuality. Just as successful brands focus on understanding their audience and building genuine connections, we as parents need to focus on understanding our children and supporting their unique journeys.

Moving Forward: Empowerment Over Projection

If there's one thing I've learned, it's that parenting isn't about perfection—it's about progress. To all the parents reading this: it's okay to reflect, admit mistakes, and start anew. Acknowledge your fears, but don't let them dictate your parenting. Instead, use them as a foundation for growth.

Start by asking yourself:
Am I parenting from a place of fear or empowerment?
Are my expectations for my child rooted in their needs or my past experiences?

How can I support their individuality while still guiding them with love and intention?
Parenting is a journey, and every day is an opportunity to rewrite the narrative—not for your child, but with them. Let's stop projecting our fears and start empowering the next generation to bloom into who they're meant to be, free of the shadows of our past.

Your children are not your second chance at life; they are their own chance to thrive. Let's give them the tools, the love, and the freedom to do just that.

The Parenting Parallel:

Think of projections like marketing a product based on outdated data. When brands rely on assumptions from the past instead of adapting to present realities, they risk misalignment with their audience. Similarly, parenting based on unresolved fears or unmet dreams can lead to misalignment with your child's true needs. To connect with their "audience" (their child), parents must approach the relationship with awareness and adaptability.

Breaking the Cycle of Projections

Identifying Triggers: Recognize moments when your fears or past experiences influence your reactions to your child's choices. Encouraging Individuality: Allow your child the freedom to explore their strengths and passions, even if they differ from what you envisioned for them.

Addressing Your Past: Work through unresolved trauma or unmet goals to prevent them from shaping your child's future.

Your Next Step:

Pause the next time you find yourself reacting strongly to a decision your child makes. Ask yourself, "Is this about their needs or my fears?" Take a moment to separate your past from their present before responding.

Reflect on This:

Are you parenting based on your child's strengths and interests, or are you unintentionally steering them based on your own past experiences? How can you better align your parenting with their unique journey?

Emotional Intelligence (EI) Insight: Navigating Projections with Self-Awareness

EI empowers parents to reflect on their emotional triggers and separate their past experiences from their child's reality. This self-awareness allows parents to approach their child with empathy and support rather than control or fear.

EI Applications for Avoiding Projections:

Self-Awareness: Identify moments when your emotions stem from your past rather than your child's present needs.

Empathy: Listen to your child's aspirations and validate their feelings, even if they differ from your own experiences.

Self-Compassion: Acknowledge your past struggles and give yourself grace for the impact they've had on your parenting.

Why EI Matters:

When parents practice Emotional Intelligence, they create space for their child to grow authentically, free from the weight of unmet parental expectations. This builds trust and allows children to develop their own identities.

Research Insight:

Dr. Gabor Maté emphasizes that parents often unconsciously project unresolved wounds onto their children, creating pressure and tension in the parent-child relationship. Healing these wounds is key to fostering healthier dynamics and nurturing a child's individuality.

Chapter 9: The Intersection of Religion, Values, and Parenting

When it comes to religion and values in parenting, one thing is clear: laying a strong foundation matters. Ideally, these conversations should take place before bringing children into the world. But let's be real life doesn't always go according to plan. Most children aren't born into perfectly pre-planned circumstances. Instead, they're often the result of passionate love, fleeting romance, or unexpected surprises.

I can't count how many times I've heard people say, "We weren't expecting it," with a grin. And while that might feel amusing in hindsight, the reality of raising a child in a home where values and religious beliefs aren't aligned is no joke. It's especially challenging when those differences rear their heads during key moments like holidays, rites of passage, or even day-to-day decisions about how to instill discipline or gratitude.

Take holidays, for instance. Some religions don't celebrate them at all, while others make them the centerpiece of family traditions. Now imagine a child raised in a home where one parent insists on ignoring Christmas, while the other decorates the house like it's Santa's personal workshop. For the child, this inconsistency creates confusion, and for the parents, it leads to conflict.

Similarly, I've seen families torn apart over dietary restrictions dictated by religious beliefs. A parent might genuinely believe they're protecting their child's well-being by enforcing strict guidelines, while the other parent might see it as unnecessary or extreme. These differences may start small but can snowball over time, causing division not just between parents, but also between the child and one or both parents.

Marketing Connection

Values, much like brands, are shaped and influenced by consistent messaging. Think of your family as a marketing team: if one parent is sending out an ad campaign for "Holiday Cheer" and the other is broadcasting "Minimalist Living," the brand confusion will affect the audience—your child.

Just like in retail, where a clear and cohesive brand identity can make or break a product, the consistency (or lack thereof) in your values will shape how your child perceives their own identity and worldview. When the messaging isn't aligned, children are left to interpret mixed signals on their own, often leading to internal conflict.

Emotional Intelligence: Navigating Differences with Empathy

When religion and values clash in parenting, emotional intelligence plays a critical role in maintaining balance and fostering respect. Here are key ways emotional intelligence can guide parents through these complex situations:

Self-Awareness: Recognize your emotional triggers around religion and values. Are you projecting your own upbringing onto your child? Are you holding onto resentment or fear because of your experiences? For example, if you were raised in a strict religious household and rebelled against it, you might unconsciously overcompensate by adopting a "free choice" approach without setting any foundation. Reflect on whether your choices are rooted in clarity or unresolved emotions.

Empathy in Action: When navigating differences in religious beliefs—whether between co-parents, grandparents, or even your child—step into their shoes. For instance, if one parent doesn't celebrate holidays due to religious beliefs, consider how that feels for your child who may be exposed to holiday celebrations in school. How can you honor their emotions while staying true to your beliefs?

Communication: Emotional intelligence thrives on clear and open dialogue. Instead of asserting dominance over religious choices, invite collaboration. Phrases like, "How do you feel about this?" or "What values do you think this teaches?" can open the door to mutual understanding and allow children to voice their thoughts.

Modeling Respect: Remember, your children are watching how you handle differences. By showing respect for different perspectives—whether it's your partner's beliefs, your parents' traditions, or your child's curiosity—you're teaching them how to navigate the complexities of the world with grace.

Flexibility vs. Foundation: Emotional intelligence helps strike the balance between instilling foundational values and allowing room for growth. Teach your children the principles you believe in but remain open to their exploration. The goal isn't to control their spiritual path but to equip them with the tools to find it.

Fostering Connection Over Compliance

Open Discussions: Create a safe space where children can ask questions and explore beliefs without fear of judgment.

Modeling Values: Children learn more from what parents do than what they say. Consistently living out your values creates a stronger connection than rigid enforcement.

Balancing Guidance and Freedom: Allow children to explore and form their own relationship with faith and values, while providing a supportive framework.

Your Next Step

To avoid confusion and tension, it's important to have honest discussions about values and religion as early as possible. If you're co-parenting or navigating these differences with extended family, set clear boundaries and agreements about how you'll present a united front to your child. And if you didn't have these conversations before the kids came along? That's okay—it's never too late to start. Focus on the values you do agree on and emphasize them as much as possible to create a stable foundation for your child to build upon.

Reflection

What are your family's core values?

Are there areas where you and your co-parent or extended family send mixed signals?

How can you align your actions to reflect the values you want to instill in your child?

Are you fostering open discussions about religion and values, or are you enforcing them in ways that may create resistance?

What kind of relationship do you want your child to have with your family's beliefs?

Emotional Intelligence (EI) Insight: Building Values Through Empathy and Curiosity

EI allows parents to approach discussions about religion and values with empathy and understanding, creating a space where children feel safe to explore their identity. Instead of demanding compliance, EI encourages connection through curiosity and open communication.

EI Applications for Religion and Values:

Empathy: Acknowledge your child's feelings and questions, even when they challenge your beliefs.

Self-Awareness: Reflect on whether your approach to teaching values stems from fear or genuine connection.

Intentional Communication: Use stories and experiences to convey the meaning behind your beliefs, rather than relying on rigid rules.

Why EI Matters:

When parents foster curiosity and connection rather than fear, they create an environment where children can develop their own moral compass while staying grounded in the family's core values.

Research Insight:

Studies from the Pew Research Center show that children who are allowed to explore their values and beliefs within a supportive framework are more likely to carry those values into adulthood.

Chapter 10: The Parent Relaunch – Designing Your Positive Parenting Campaign

I think everyone, at some point, has wished for a "do-over." If I were granted one wish from a magical genie, this would undoubtedly be mine. But since life doesn't work that way, I've learned to embrace the concept of relaunching. Writing this book has been part of my relaunch.

As I write this, my daughter is 18, my son is 24, and my husband and I are celebrating 20 years of marriage, having been together for 27 years in total as of 2025. Reflecting on the journey of parenting has been both humbling and enlightening. It's made me realize that while we may not get the chance to start over, we can always evolve, refine, and implement new strategies.

Parenting doesn't come with a playbook, but it does offer the chance to constantly relaunch our approach and adapt as needed. Think of this relaunch like running a marketing campaign. Every successful campaign goes through a process of A/B testing—trying different approaches to see what resonates best with the target audience. In parenting, our "audience" is our children, and they change over time. What worked for a five-year-old may not work for a teenager, and what works for one child may not work for another. The key is to remain flexible, observant, and open to adjustments.

Parenting in Action:

When my son was younger, I thought strict routines and firm discipline were the answer to everything. It worked—for a while. But as he grew older, I realized those methods didn't resonate with the person he was becoming. I had to pivot, learning how to listen more, loosen the reins, and adapt my parenting style. With my daughter, I took a different approach from the start, applying lessons learned with her brother. Even then, I found myself adjusting again and again as she transitioned from childhood to adolescence.

The Importance of Checkpoints

In marketing, checkpoints are essential. They allow you to measure progress, evaluate what's working, and determine what needs to be adjusted. This also allows you to course-correct as quickly as possible without allowing too much time to pass. As parents, we need similar checkpoints in our journey.

- Take time to pause and reflect:
- Are your children thriving emotionally and mentally?

- Are the strategies you're using fostering connection or creating distance?
- Have you solicited honest feedback from your children?

These checkpoints don't mean we're failing; they mean we're committed to getting it right. Parenting is not about perfection but about progress.

Embracing a Growth Mindset

One of the most liberating truths I've embraced is that it's never too late to grow as a parent. Just like brands adapt to changing markets, parents can adapt to the evolving needs of their children. Growth requires humility, an openness to feedback, and the willingness to try again.

There were times I felt like I had messed up beyond repair. The arguments I had with my son or daughter, the times I was too busy or distracted for either of them, the mistakes my husband and I made as a parenting team—they all left scars. But they also left lessons. And the lesson I hold closest is that love, accountability, and effort can heal almost anything.

Your Parenting Campaign

The idea of designing a parenting campaign might sound clinical, but it's incredibly practical. Campaigns are built around objectives, strategies, and messaging that resonate. Here's how you can apply this concept:

1. Set Your Objectives

What kind of relationship do you want with your child?
What values do you want to instill?
How do you want your home to feel?

2. Develop Your Strategies?

What tools and methods will you use? (Books, therapy, quality time?)
How will you adapt your approach as your child grows?
What will you do differently from your own upbringing?

3. Refine Your Messaging

Are your words and actions aligned?
How are you showing your love and support?
What are you repeating through your actions that will stick with your child for life?

4. Evaluate and Relaunch

Regularly assess how things are going.
Celebrate wins, acknowledge setbacks, and adjust accordingly.

Key Performance Indicators (KPIs) for Parenting

Borrowing from marketing, KPIs provide measurable benchmarks to evaluate and improve parenting approaches. By defining clear objectives and tracking progress, parents can intentionally foster a positive, nurturing environment.

Framework for Parenting KPIs

1. **Objective**: Define the parenting goal.

2. **Key Performance Indicator**: Identify the measurable action or behavior tied to the goal.

3. **Frequency**: Establish how often the action should occur.

4. **Measurement**: Determine how progress will be tracked.

5. **Adjustment**: Reflect on outcomes and adjust strategies as needed.

Examples of Parenting KPIs

1. Emotional Presence

- **Objective**: Strengthen your child's sense of emotional security.

- **Key Performance Indicator**: Spend undivided, distraction-free time with your child.

- **Frequency**: 15 minutes daily.

- **Measurement**: Maintain a journal to note the quality of time spent (e.g., reading together, having a meaningful conversation, playing a game).

- **Adjustment**: If daily time is difficult, shift to a realistic weekly target while ensuring consistency.

2. Positive Reinforcement

- **Objective**: Build your child's self-esteem and foster positive behaviors.

- **Key Performance Indicator**: Provide specific, positive affirmations or acknowledgments.

- **Frequency**: At least three affirmations per day.

- **Measurement**: Use a checklist or app to track affirmations and note your child's response.

- **Adjustment**: If affirmations feel repetitive, diversify by focusing on different achievements, traits, or efforts.

3. Conflict Resolution

- **Objective**: Model healthy problem-solving skills.

- **Key Performance Indicator**: Demonstrate calm and constructive conflict resolution in challenging situations.

- **Frequency**: At least one instance weekly.

- **Measurement**: Reflect in a journal or during family check-ins on how conflicts were resolved and how the child reacted.

- **Adjustment**: If unresolved conflicts persist, seek feedback from family members and adjust strategies to improve communication.

4. Family Connection

- **Objective**: Create a sense of belonging and shared purpose.

- **Key Performance Indicator**: Plan and participate in a family activity.

- **Frequency**: One activity per week.

- **Measurement**: Keep a family calendar to document activities and gather feedback from family members on what they enjoyed.

- **Adjustment**: Experiment with different activities to find what resonates most with your family.

5. Open Communication

- **Objective**: Foster trust and emotional expression.
- **Key Performance Indicator**: Have a meaningful check-in conversation with your child.
- **Frequency**: Once per week.
- **Measurement**: Track topics discussed and note whether the child initiated conversations or expressed feelings more openly over time.
- **Adjustment**: If conversations feel forced, try changing the setting (e.g., talking during a walk or drive) or ask open-ended questions to spark dialogue.

Implementation Plan

1. **Start Small**: Choose one or two KPIs to focus on initially.
2. **Track Progress**: Use tools like journals, apps, or family charts to monitor consistency and effectiveness.
3. **Involve Your Child**: Share your goals with your child and invite their feedback. This fosters accountability and helps them feel included.
4. **Reflect and Adjust**: Periodically review your progress and make adjustments based on outcomes and feedback from your child or partner.

Why KPIs Work in Parenting

- **Clarity**: Establishes clear goals and actionable steps.
- **Consistency**: Encourages regular habits that build trust and connection.

- **Growth-Oriented**: Promotes reflection and continuous improvement.

- **Empowering**: Demonstrates to children that parenting is a journey of learning and growth.

Reflection

If you could relaunch one aspect of your parenting, what would it be? Take a moment to reflect on what you've learned from your mistakes and how those lessons can shape your future relationship with your children.

Emotional Intelligence Insight

Relaunching requires emotional intelligence—understanding not only your children's needs but also your own triggers and behaviors. Be honest with yourself about what drives your actions and where you can grow.

Next Steps

1. Reflect and Reset

Take 10 minutes today to reflect in one area of your parenting that you'd like to relaunch. Write it down.

2. Create a Plan

Use the steps in this chapter to outline your parenting campaign. Set realistic goals and timelines for change.

3. Start Small

Choose one actionable change to implement this week. Share your plan with your child or partner for accountability.

4. Celebrate Progress

Acknowledge small victories as they come. Growth is a journey, not a destination.

Start your relaunch today. Write down one thing you want to change in your parenting approach. Then, create a simple action plan for how to implement that change. Share your intention with your child if they're old enough—it's okay to let them know you're growing too. Relaunching doesn't mean you failed. It means you're willing to do the work to build something better. And that, more than anything, is what your children will remember.

Bonus Section: The Parenting Toolbox – Resources for Success

Parenting doesn't come with a manual, but it can come with a toolbox. This bonus section is designed to provide practical resources and actionable strategies to help you take your parenting journey to the next level. From emotional intelligence exercises to family rituals that foster connection, this toolbox equips you with tools to build a strong, nurturing environment for your children.

Tool 1: Emotional Intelligence (EI) Exercises for Parents
Developing EI is a game-changer in parenting. It helps you regulate your emotions, connect with your child on a deeper level, and model healthy emotional behaviors.

Name the Feeling: When you or your child is upset, take a moment to name the emotion out loud. For example, say, "I'm feeling frustrated because I'm running late." This normalizes emotional expression and teaches your child to identify their own feelings.

Pause and Breathe: Before reacting to a stressful situation, take three deep breaths. Use this moment to reflect on your response and choose a calm, thoughtful approach.

Gratitude Journaling: At the end of each day, write down three things you're grateful for. Share one of them with your child during bedtime to reinforce positive thinking.

Tool 2: Family Connection Rituals

Creating consistent rituals fosters a sense of belonging and security.

Weekly Family Meetings: Set aside time each week to discuss highs, lows, and plans as a family. This encourages communication and ensures everyone feels heard.

Daily Affirmations: Start each morning with a family affirmation, such as, "Today, we will be kind, brave, and supportive."

Memory Jar: Keep a jar where family members can drop notes about fun moments or achievements. Read them together at the end of the year.

Tool 3: Conversation Starters for Deeper Communication

Use these prompts to encourage meaningful dialogue with your children:

"What made you smile today?"

"If you could do anything tomorrow, what would it be?"

"What's one thing you're proud of this week?"

Tool 4: Family Goal-Setting Worksheets

Use guided worksheets to set goals as a family. For example: Family Values Worksheet: Write down three values you want to prioritize (e.g., kindness, honesty, teamwork) and brainstorm ways to embody them daily.

Individual Growth Plan: Encourage each family member to set one personal goal and share how they'll work toward it.

Bonus Chapter: The Unseen Curriculum – Modeling Life Beyond Parenting

Parenting doesn't stop with how we interact with our children directly; it extends to the subtle lessons they pick up by observing how we navigate life. From how we treat our friends and handle work responsibilities to our cleaning habits and communication styles, our children are always watching. For work-from-home parents, the lines blur even further, making every moment an unintentional lesson in responsibility, authority, and relationships.

Compelling Narrative:

I once spoke with a mother whose child proudly told a friend, "My mom is the boss of her own meetings!" She was amused but also struck by the realization: her child wasn't just learning about professionalism from her words but from observing how she interacted with colleagues and handled stress during her work-from-home days.

Parenting in Action:

Imagine a child who grows up seeing their parent treat friends with kindness and loyalty. They're more likely to approach their own friendships with similar values. On the other hand, a child who witnesses a parent avoid conflict or dismiss responsibilities may unknowingly adopt those habits as well.

The Parenting Parallel:

Think of this as brand exposure. In marketing, consumers don't just form opinions based on direct advertising—they observe the brand's interactions with others, its consistency, and its authenticity. Similarly, children learn about authority, responsibility, and interpersonal dynamics by observing how their parents "present their brand" to the world.

Content: Setting the Tone for the Future

Friendship Values: How you treat your friends influences your child's understanding of loyalty, honesty, and boundaries.
Work Habits: Children pick up on how you handle stress, authority, and collaboration, shaping their views on professionalism.
Daily Routines: Even mundane tasks like cleaning and organizing teach your child about responsibility and pride in one's environment.

Your Next Step:

Observe your own interactions this week—whether with friends, colleagues, or your environment. Ask yourself what messages your child might be taking from these moments and how you can align your actions with the lessons you want them to learn.

Series Roadmap: Building a Legacy of Empowered Parenting

This book is just the beginning of a larger journey to uncover the unseen forces shaping our children. Together, we'll explore not just what they remember and see, but the hidden lessons they absorb every day. Parenting isn't about perfection—it's about awareness, intention, and growth.

Let's keep walking this path together. Each step will bring us closer to building the legacy we want to leave for our children. The next book, What They See Is Who They'll Be, will take us further into understanding how our everyday actions influence their friendships, work ethic, and overall approach to life. And then, in The Hidden Curriculum of Parenting, we'll dive even deeper, illuminating the silent messages that shape their identity and worldview.

Next in the Journey: What They See Is Who They'll Be

Children don't just learn from what we say—they absorb how we live. Every interaction, every habit, every response we model becomes a building block for their future relationships, career choices, and life skills.

In What They See Is Who They'll Be, we'll explore the nuanced ways our actions shape their understanding of friendships, authority, and responsibility. From how we manage stress at work to how we treat strangers in public, our behavior becomes their blueprint.

Through relatable stories and actionable insights, this next release will guide parents toward intentional living that sets their children up for success—not just in childhood, but throughout their lives.

This book will include:

Friendship Foundations: What your child learns from how you handle loyalty, disagreements, and boundaries.

Work Ethic & Boundaries: The lessons you teach about perseverance, balance, and self-respect through your own work habits.

Everyday Interactions: How your treatment of others—be it a neighbor or a cashier—teaches respect, empathy, and emotional intelligence.

Get ready to reflect, recalibrate, and reimagine your role in shaping who your children will become. Stay tuned for What They See Is Who They'll Be.

Unlocking the Hidden Curriculum of Parenting

Parenting isn't just about what we teach—it's about what we model, even without realizing it. From unspoken cultural norms to hidden biases, children absorb lessons we never intended to teach. These silent messages shape their identity, values, and worldview in profound ways.

In The Hidden Curriculum of Parenting, we'll uncover the unseen forces influencing our children's lives. How do cultural expectations, unconscious habits, and even our unspoken emotions shape their understanding of themselves and the world? More importantly, how can we rewrite these lessons to create a more intentional, empowered future?

This next release will dive into topics such as:
Unconscious Bias and Cultural Norms: The subtle messages children pick up from what's left unsaid.
Breaking Cycles of Privilege or Scarcity: How our perspectives on success, struggle, or failure shape their worldview.
Rewriting the Rules: Practical steps to identify and reshape unintentional parenting patterns.

With The Hidden Curriculum of Parenting, we'll shine a light on the silent lessons shaping our children—and provide the tools to rewrite them for the better. This book is for parents who want to go beyond the obvious and delve into the deeper dynamics at play.

Connect and Stay Updated

This series is about progress, not perfection. It's about creating a parenting legacy that inspires resilience, emotional intelligence, and love in future generations. To stay updated on these upcoming books, visit www.moniquecorker.com and join our community of parents striving for intentional change.

Let's continue this journey together—one chapter, one moment, and one breakthrough at a time.

References

Center on the Developing Child at Harvard University. (n.d.). The science of early childhood development. Retrieved from https://developingchild.harvard.edu

Goleman, D. (1995). Emotional intelligence: Why it can matter more than IQ. Bantam Books.

Maté, G. (2019). The myth of normal: Trauma, illness, and healing in a toxic culture. Avery Publishing.

Pew Research Center. (2022). Parenting in America today. Retrieved from https://www.pewresearch.org

Shonkoff, J. P., & Phillips, D. A. (2000). From neurons to neighborhoods: The science of early childhood development. National Academies Press.

Brookings Institution. (2020). Financial education and inclusion: Why teaching kids about money matters. Retrieved from https://www.brookings.edu

American Psychological Association. (n.d.). Parenting and family relationships. Retrieved from https://www.apa.org

Cialdini, R. B. (2001). Influence: The psychology of persuasion. Harper Business.

Keller, K. L. (2013). Strategic brand management: Building, measuring, and managing brand equity. Pearson Education.

Made in the USA
Middletown, DE
03 February 2025